A Waldorf Song Book

A Waldorf Song Book

Collected and edited by
Brien Masters

Floris Books

Music handwritten by Jenny Wellman
Illustrations by Astrid Maclean

Front cover photography: Rebecca Landy,
with special thanks to the children of Class 3,
Briar Hill Primary School, Melbourne, Australia

First published in 1987 by Floris Books
This second edition published in 2015

British Library CIP Data is available

ISBN 978-178250-170-1

Printed and bound by Gutenberg Press Limited, Malta

Contents

Introduction

A healthy social life often finds people singing together. And conversely, singing together often assists in a healthier social life. I hope, therefore, that this collection of songs for children aged 8–14 will serve the social life of the classroom as much as it will the education of each individual. It is dedicated to all colleagues and pupils who may find it useful, in the hope that good use may lead to enjoyment, and that enjoyment may lead to many significant musical discoveries.

Ideally, in Waldorf Schools, class teachers accompany their group of children for eight years, having received them at age 6. They are responsible for teaching academic subjects such as maths or English (or the mother tongue), history and geography, and others such as mythology, astronomy, Old Testament stories, hygiene, and so on.

Although there will usually be a music specialist on the staff, it often falls to the class teacher to introduce simple songs as part of daily activities at the beginning of and during the main lesson.

This selection has been made with that particular task in mind, though it may well be that teachers of English as a foreign language, and others, will find it a useful resource.

The songs are broadly 'graded' chapter by chapter so that the pupils and teacher can take them in their musical stride. They are mostly in keys that lend themselves to recorder playing, which is a common activity in Waldorf as well as other schools. In later years, other instruments may well be brought in for accompaniment, particularly for the part-songs. The grading is naturally only a guide and is intended to be taken in that spirit.

These songs are also meant to stand on their own melodic ground without the use of any accompaniment, even though (as in Gluck's 'Che faro senza Euridice', for instance) several have important accompaniments in the original. This is not to imply that someone with the necessary ability should not add an appropriate accompaniment, either by reference to the full score, by improvising, or by devising something that the pupils themselves could manage.

At the same time, a certain stress has been laid on rounds and simple part-songs from age 9–10 upwards. The range of difficulty offered should make it possible for all classes to experience the creation of harmony together.

There are also other categories into which the songs fall.

Firstly, there are songs whose subject may be associated with suggestions Rudolf Steiner made for the Waldorf curriculum. Into this category fall 'Ein Feste Burg' (history of the Reformation); 'The Whirling Mill' (farming);

'Sigurd and the Dragon' (Norse mythology) and many others.

Secondly, there are songs in foreign languages, particularly those languages not normally taught in schools – for instance Sanskrit, Manx, Quechan, and so on. This acknowledges, at least in token, that the whole of humanity has contributed towards our wealth of culture. It is particularly important to cultivate such a multicultural attitude in our present-day society.

Thirdly, each chapter includes a few well-known songs, such as 'The Skye Boat Song', Milton's 'Let us with a Gladsome Mind' (to the tune 'Monkland'); and, amongst the rounds, 'Come Follow, Follow', 'Shalom Chaverim' and Byrd's 'Non Nobis Domine'.

Fourthly, there are also songs in each chapter which stem from the work of the Waldorf movement itself. These often arise from the specific need of a group. That they could be included here is gratefully acknowledged.

As in recitation, so in singing, one of the greatest needs of the teacher is for material that reflects the mood of nature, season by season, culminating often in one of the major religious festivals. This is recognised in the book in so far as the structure of each chapter begins with autumn/Michaelmas. It is hoped that teachers in the southern hemisphere will find that particular orientation acceptable.

In the earliest part of the song book, the tempo and expression indications for each song are in English, except for the more obvious *p*, *f*, *cres*, and so on. From age 10–11 the usual Italian terminology is gradually introduced as part of the pupil's general music education.

One technicality needs to be clarified. Rounds are such that the usual sign for a pause (⌒) is irrelevant. Where this sign is found over a note in any of the rounds, therefore, it indicates the point during the round where each voice should stop singing in order to synchronise the ending. As round singing is very familiar today, it is hoped that this will be sufficient guidance for teachers.

Finally I would like to draw attention to the notes which tell a little about each song. These are not at all scholastically exhaustive, but are intended to give teachers ideas for introducing the songs.

Brien Masters

Class 3

From Age 8

1. Step We Gaily

Lewis Bridal Song

A joyful folk song from the Isle of Lewis to get the school year off to a good start. The rowan tree, which features in the second verse, also appears in the legend of St Bride.

2. Red her cheeks as rowans are
   Bright her eye as any star
   Fairest of them all by far
   Is our darling Mairie.

3. Plenty herring, plenty meal,
   Plenty peat to fill her creel,
   Plenty bonny bairns as weel,
   That's our toast for Mairie.

2. Unconquered Hero of the Skies

A Michaelmas song

This song unites Michaelic verse with a melody that is happily within the pentatonic range.

With firmness

1. Un-con-quer'd he- ro of the skies, Saint Mi- cha-el——

—— ; A- gainst the foe with us a- rise, *Thine aid we pray the*

foe to slay, Saint Mi———— cha-el————.

2. The heavenly banner thou dost bear, Saint Michael;
   The angels do thine armour wear;
      Thine aid we pray the foe to slay, Saint Michael.

3. Great is thy might, strong is thy hand, Saint Michael;
   Great o'er the sea, great o'er the land;
      Thine aid we pray the foe to slay, Saint Michael.

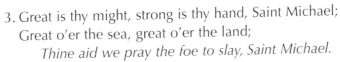

3. Green Lies the Dancing Water

The rhythm of this dynamic song is evocative of the isles off the west coast of Scotland. Their landscape is its inspiration.

Smoothly

Green lies the danc-ing wa- ter, Green, pur-ple barr'd with gold;

Brown wing'd my boat flies o'er her, Brown wing'd, while

out the wa-ter; White the keel, the curl- ing wave-let

toss- es high, spray- ing round ————.

4. Heaven Blue

Originally written for a christening, this song was inspired by an evensong.

5. Let Us with a Gladsome Mind

Words by John Milton

Poet John Milton wrote these words as an adolescent in 1623, just before the onset of the Industrial Revolution. The accompanying tune 'Monkland' appeared much later in 1824 when England was overcome with 'dark, satanic mills'. Here, two rays of light – words and music – shine through the factory smoke.

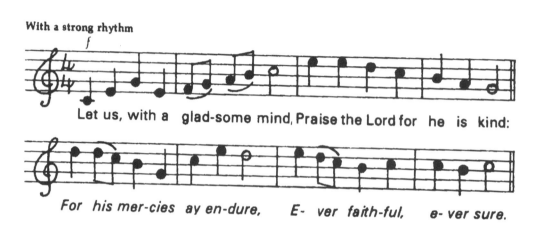

2. Let us blaze his name abroad,
  For of gods he is the God:
    For his mercies ay endure,
    Ever faithful, ever sure.

3. He with all-commanding might
  Filled the new-made world with light:

4. He the golden tressed sun
  Caused all day his course to run:

5. The horned moon to shine by night,
  'Mid her spangled sisters bright:

6. All things living he doth fee,
  His full hand supplies their need:

7. Let us, with a gladsome mind,
  Praise the Lord, for he is kind:

14

6. The Shepherd's Song

Usher in the Christmas season with this gentle carol. Its pentatonic melody lends it to class improvisation with Orff instruments such as the glockenspiel and chimes.

Lightly

mp

Once upon a starry midnight Stood I up-on a mountain Silver-grey the silent sheep

Slumbering, slumbering, Slumbering so deep, A- mong the hills so fair.

2. Quietly the vault above me
   Opened like the rose in summer:
       Rainbow light streamed through its crown
       Glimmering, glistening,
       Jewelling all down
   Among the hills so fair.

3. Winging through the midnight splendour
   Angels with chanting voices
       Songs of joy and songs of birth
       Carolling, carolling:
       Joy to all the earth,
   Among the hills so fair.

4. Gladly then I turned my footsteps
   Down to the straw-bright cradle;
       There I danced with heart-filled glee,
       Merrily, merrily,
       Merry-merrily,
   Among the hills so fair.

7. Skye Boat Song

Spark the class's imagination with this lilting tune, which describes Bonnie Prince Charlie's escape to Skye after his defeat in the Battle of Culloden in 1746.

With a gentle lilt

Speed, bon-ny boat, like a bird on the wing,

"On-ward" the sail-ors cry. Car-ry the lad that's

born to be king, O- ver the sea to Skye. Skye

1. Loud the winds howl, loud the waves roar,
2. Though the waves leap, soft shall ye sleep,

Thun-der-claps rend the air. Ba-ffled our foes
O-cean's a roy-al bed. Rock'd in the deep,

stand by the shore, Fol- low they will not dare. *(Chorus)*
Flo- ra will keep Watch by your wea-ry head. *(Chorus)*

8. The Whirling Mill

An excellent accompaniment to a lesson on farming or a craft activity, this song reflects the important connection we have to our daily work. These words were unearthed by the Sussex Archaeological Society.

tempo primo

And facing windward straight and true, straight and true,

It does the work it finds to do, it finds to do,

The wheat, the barley, sun-embrown'd, To white & snowy meal are ground,

ritardando

And ho! the wind sings blithe- ly through——————

The whirl- ing mill.

9. On this, our Glorious Eastertide

There is an implicit dance rhythm in this Dutch folk song with its heavy, cloglike two in a bar. At the same time, a strong, liberated, uplifting note of joy captures the hope of the Easter festival.

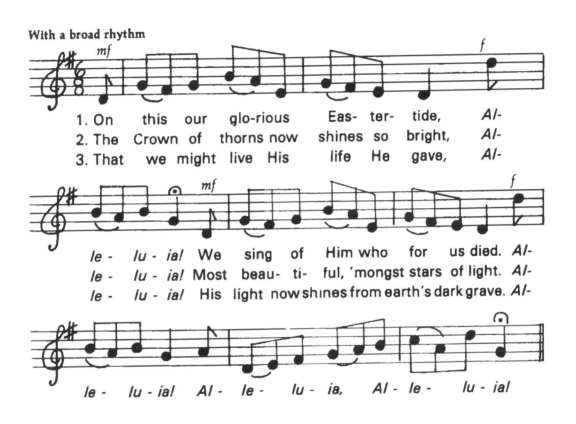

With a broad rhythm

1. On this our glo-rious Eas- ter- tide, Al-
2. The Crown of thorns now shines so bright, Al-
3. That we might live His life He gave, Al-

le - lu - ia! We sing of Him who for us died. Al-
le - lu - ia! Most beau- ti- ful, 'mongst stars of light. Al-
le - lu - ia! His light now shines from earth's dark grave. Al-

le - lu - ia! Al - le - lu - ia, Al - le - lu - ia!

10. This Joyful Easter Day

For Easter Sunday – music by Adrian Willaert; words by Catherine von Alphen

Radiantly

1. This joy-ful Eas-ter Day, The sun has pierc'd the
And with his shin-ing ray, Re- veals to us his

clouds of night ———————;
wond-rous light ——————.

CHORUS

And like the seed that

grows from ev'r-y flow'r that dies ———————; More

ra-diant than the rose. Let love in Man a-

- rise ———, a - rise ———, a - rise ———, Let

love in Man a - rise ———————

2. The corn is milled for bread
   Grain glowing once, in glowing sun;
   Each deed on earth a thread,
   That may in web of life be spun.
   (Chorus)

3. The grape is pressed for wine;
   The broken branch sends forth a shoot;
   The jewel lies in the mine;
   The hollow reed becomes a flute.
   (Chorus)

11. Over the Hills and Far Away

This song derives from *The Beggar's Opera* by John Gay. It achieved such popularity on its first performance in 1728 that it challenged even Handel's success. Its simple ballad form appealed to the nation's taste for hearty folk tunes.

12. The Dawn Wind Now is Waking

A Béarnaise summer carol

Welcome in spring with this delightful French tune, whose intervening 2/4 bars give it a distinct, free character. The freshness of dawn is also captured in Geoffrey Dearmer's words, as if he had painted it himself.

2. Now quickly goes the grey light;
   Aslant, the sun redeems
   A whole long day of daylight;
   Gold crowd a wealth of beams.
   Chickens flutter, strut and babble;
   Running ducks the duck-pond fill;
   Early breezes bear the gabble,
   And the light increases till
   Soon it finds beyond the rabble
   The blackbird's yellow bill.

3. Bright flow'rs the woods adorning
   Show earth's no longer blind,
   As once on Christmas morning,
   When snow the world did bind,
   When the shepherds and the sages
   And the kings first met their King,
   Brought him wisdom, wealth, and wages,
   Though he was their littlest thing;
   Suddenly the iron ages
   Had yielded to the spring.

13. Little Red Bird of the Lonely Moor

A Manx lullaby

The desolation of the peat moor and the rugged beauty of the Isle of Man's landscape echo in the modal melody of this folk song. The little bird in question is probably a redstart.

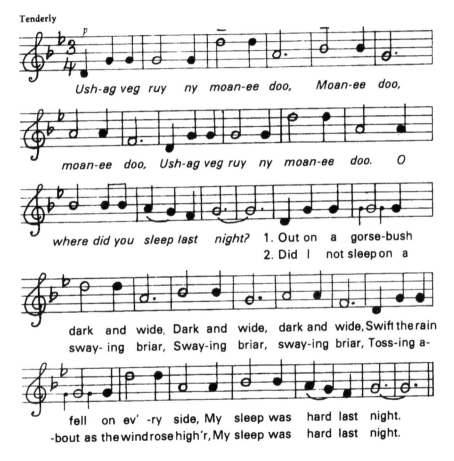

Tenderly

Ush-ag veg ruy ny moan-ee doo, Moan-ee doo,

moan-ee doo, Ush-ag veg ruy ny moan-ee doo. O

where did you sleep last night?
1. Out on a gorse-bush
2. Did I not sleep on a

dark and wide, Dark and wide, dark and wide, Swift the rain
sway-ing briar, Sway-ing briar, sway-ing briar, Toss-ing a-

fell on ev'-ry side, My sleep was hard last night.
-bout as the wind rose high'r, My sleep was hard last night.

(Chorus)
3. Did I not sleep on a cold wave's crest,
   Cold wave's crest, cold wave's crest,
   Where many a man has taken his rest?
   My sleep was hard last night.

(Chorus)
4. Wrapped in two leaves I lay at ease,
   Lay at ease, lay at ease,
   As sleeps the young babe on its mother's knees
   My sleep was sweet last night.

14. Down in the Valley

An Austrian shepherd's song

There is a touch of the Alps about this folk melody that rides happily in tandem with Laurence Binyon's description of the sheep being dipped.

With rustic gaiety

mf 1. Down in the val- ley where sum- mer's laugh-ing beam
f 2. Ah, how they strug-gle, and pant, the sil- ly sheep,
p 3. Eve- ning is o- ver the land, with peace and light,

Un- der the wil- low tree lights a- long the stream,
Fear-ing the hands that dip, fear- ing wa- ter deep.
Now sits the shep-herd a- lone in eve- ning bright,

Shep-herds come driv- ing their flocks and seek the pool,
Ten- der -ly lift- ed up, glad- ly, one by one,
Now has he joy with-in, where he pi- peth low,

Plung-ing their sheep in the sun- ny wa- ter cool.
White in the green of the mea- dow, lo, they run.
See- ing his flock gath-er'd round him white as snow.

15. How Beautiful They Are, the Lordly Ones

The Immortal Hour, an opera by Rutland Boughton (1878–1960), was performed at the Glastonbury summer festival of August 1914. It was hoped that the performance would bring about a modest renewal of interest in Arthurian culture.

16. How Delightful to See

A sheep-shearing song from Somerset

Folk music has received a resurgence of attention in the music world since the end of the eighteenth century. Cecil Sharp and his associates were instrumental in bringing a wealth of this material back to a wide audience.

2. The sixth month of the year,
   In the month callèd June
   When the weather's too hot to be borne,
   The master doth say,
   As he goes on his way:
   "Tomorrow my sheep shall be shorn,
   Tomorrow my sheep shall be shorn."

3. Now the sheep they're all shorn,
   And the wool carried home;
   Here's a health to our master and flock;
   And if we should stay
   Till the last goes away,
   I'm afraid 'twill be past twelve o'clock,
   I'm afraid 'twill be past twelve o'clock.

17. Once on a Bright Summer's Day

Raphael's and other Renaissance painters' work abounds in depictions of the two cousins, Jesus and John, but seldom do they appear in literature. This naïve exception, including a second verse added for St John's Tide, celebrates birth rather than martyrdom.

Quickly, but not breathlessly

1. And once up-on a time on a bright sum-mer's day, I saw two boys and a lamb at play; Our little Je-sus and St John A-way into the fields they've gone; One car-ries a por-rin- ger in his hand, As they walk through the clo- ver and but-ter-cup land.

2. And when the sum-mer fad- ed and dark was the land Those two stood to- geth-er on Jor-dan's strand; With waters blue as heav'ns above, On hov'ring wings there came the dove; While John baptiz'd Jesus, came God's voice so free: "This day have I be- got- ten Thee."

18. The Ash Grove

Llwyn On (Welsh)

This song provides a celebration of the strength of Welsh music. The bardic tradition has enjoyed greater public awareness recently – long may its revival last.

Very tunefully

1. The ash grove how grace-ful, how plain-ly 'tis
1. Yn Mhal-as Llwyn On gynt, fi drig-ai pen-

speaking, The wind thro' it play-ing has lan-guage for
def-ig, Ef e oedd ys- gwei-ar ac ar- glwydd y

me; When o- ver its branches the sunlight is breaking, A
wiad; Ac idd- o un en-eth a an-wyd yn un-ig, A

host of kind fa- ces is gaz-ing on me. The
hi 'nol yr han- es oedd aer- es ei thad. Aeth

friends of my child-hood a- gain are be- fore me, Fond
Car- iad i'w gwel- ed, yn idn a phar lenc-yn, Ond

me- mo- ries wa- ken as free- ly I roam, With
cod- ai'r ys- gwei-ar yn af- ar ac erch, I

soft whis-pers la- den its leaves rus-tle o'er me, The
saeth-u'r bach- gen- yn, ond gwŷr-odd ei lin-yn, A'i

ash grove, the ash grove that shel-ter'd my home.
er- gyd yn wyr-gam i fyn- wes ei ferch.

2. My laughter is over, my step loses lightness,
　　Old countryside measures steal soft on mine ear;
I only remember the past and its brightness,
　　The dear ones I mourn for again gather here.
From out of the shadows their loving looks greet me,
　　And wistfully searching the leafy green dome,
I find other faces fond bending me greet me:
　　The ash grove, the ash grove alone is my home!

2. *Ryh hwyr ydoedd galw y saeth at y llinyn,*
　　A'r llances yn marw yn welw a gwan;
Bygythiodd ei gleddyf trwy galon y llencyn;
　　Ond ni redai Cariad un fodfedd o'r fan.
'Roedd Golud, ei "darpar" yn hèn ac anynad,
　　A geiriau diweddaf yr Aeres hardd hon,
Oedd, "gwell genyf farw trwy ergyd fy Nghariad
　　Na byw gyda Golud yn Mhalas Llwyn On."

19. The Flowers in the Valley

Children love the colourful imagery and gloriously free melody of this folk song.

2. There came a knight all clothed in red,
   Fair are the flowers in the valley;
   "I would thou wert my bride," he said,
   The Red, the Green, and the Yellow.
   The harp, the lute, the pipe, the flute, the cymbal,
   Sweet goes the treble violin:
   "I would," she sighed, "ne'er wins a bride!"
   Fair are the flowers in the valley.

3. There came a knight all clothed in green,
   Fair are the flowers in the valley;
   "This maid so sweet might be my queen,"
   The Red, the Green, and the Yellow.
   The harp, the lute, the pipe, the flute, the cymbal,
   Sweet goes the treble violin:
   "Might be," sighed she, "will ne'er win me!"
   Fair are the flowers in the valley.

4. There came a knight, in yellow was he,
   Fair are the flowers in the valley;
   "My bride, my queen, thou must with me!"
   The Red, the Green, and the Yellow.
   The harp, the lute, the pipe, the flute, the cymbal,
   Sweet goes the treble violin:
   With blushes red, "I come," she said;
   "Farewell to the flowers in the valley."

20. Waken Sleeping Butterfly

Birthday song

Tom Scratchley composed this lively birthday song for a young class in Edinburgh.

With a rocking rhythm

1. Wa- ken sleep- ing but- ter- fly, Burst —
2. Birth- day sun break through the clouds, Shine —

— your nar- row pri- son;
— on joy and sor- row;

Spread your gol - den wings and fly
Life and light for earth to- day;

For the sun has ri - sen.
Star of love to- mor - row.

21. The Merry Haymakers

From the West Country

Flowing happily

mf

1. The gol-den sun is shin- ing bright, The

dew is off the field; To us it is our

main de-light The fork and rake to wield.

f

The pipe and ta- bor both shall play, The

vi- ols loud- ly ring, From morn till eve each

DC al $·

sum-mer day, As we go hay- mak- ing.

2. As we, my boys, haymaking go,
   All in the month of June,
   Both Tom and Bet, and Jess and Joe,
   Their happy hearts in tune.
   Oh up come sturdy Jack and Will,
   With pitchfork and with rake,
   And up come dainty Doll and Jill,
   The sweet, sweet hay to make.
   The pipe and tabor...

3. Oh when the haysel all is done,
   Then in the arish grass,
   The lads shall have their fill of fun,
   Each dancing with his lass.
   The good old farmer and his wife
   Shall bring the best of cheer,
   I would it were, aye, odds my life!
   Haymaking all the year.
   The pipe and tabor...

Class 4

From Age 9

22. Sigurd and the Dragon

A Faeroese folk song

This song makes a vivid accompaniment to a lesson on Norse mythology. The legend of the Edda is at the root of northern culture, and in this version Sigurd's slaying of the dragon is recounted in a powerful folk melody.

1. Come, good peop-le, lis- ten now, Lis- ten to my sto- ry
2. It was Si-gurd brave and bold, Rode the heath of Glit- ra.

Of the rich and migh-ty kings And their deeds of glo-
'Gainst the one who meets his sword He will show no pi-

-ry. Gra- ni brought gold from the heath O. Gra-
-ty.

-ni bar gull av hei- di. Brá hann si- num bran-

-di av rei- di. Si- gurd struck the dra- gon dead.

Gra- ni bar gul- lid av hei- di!

3. On the gold the dragon lies,
    Shrieking loud in vengeance.
    Sigurd sits on Grani's back,
    With his sword he threatens.
        Grani brought gold from the heath O.

5. It was Sigurd brave and bold,
    He his sword did brandish;
    In two parts asunder lay
    Dead the glitt'ring dragon. *(Chorus)*

4. Sigurd gave so big a thrust,
    'Twas a mighty wonder;
    Trembled both the leaves and trees
    As though struck by thunder. *(Chorus)*

(Alternative English chorus)
Gold from the heath he brought O,
Swung his sword with rage and anger.
Sigurd struck the dragon dead.
Grani brought gold from the heath O.

23. Happy Birthday

A round in three parts

In Waldorf Schools, rounds and descants are introduced at this stage. A birthday round can quickly become a favourite in the class repertoire.

37

24. Reap the Flax

Swedish reaping song

Flax, from field to wardrobe, takes as much hard labour as it does delicate skill. This traditional song describes some of the processes, and is a good accompaniment to craft activities.

1. Come, har-vest now the ripe flax to- day, Card, card it well, and spin, spin a-way.
2. Come, now the flax we're card-ing to- day, Card, card it well, and spin, spin a-way.

Soon we will weave our costumes so gay, Then off we go a- danc-ing.
Soon we will weave our costumes so gay, Then off we go a- danc-ing.

Doonk, doonk, doonk, doonk, doonk, doonk, Spools whirl a-round, spools whirl a-round.

Doonk, doonk, doonk, doonk, doonk, doonk, Then off we go a- danc- ing.

3. Come, now the flax we're spinning today,
   Carded so well, we spin, spin away.
   Soon we will weave our costumes so gay,
   Then off we go a-dancing.
      Doonk, doonk, etc.

4. Now finest cloth we're weaving today,
   Spinning is done, we weave, weave away
   Soon we will weave our costumes so gay,
   And lightly swing in dancing.
      Doonk, doonk, etc.

25. The Frosty Air is Echoing

A huntsman's song

Originally named 'A Song of Anderida', this song is an excellent accompaniment to an outdoor activity, as it describes wild woodland pursuits in the ancient forests.

Rousing but not rowdy

1. The fros- ty air is e- cho-ing with bu- gle clear the
The king and all his fol- low-ers are rid- ing forth to

live- long day, All the merry woods are glad To
seek their prey. Of the horses' pounding hoofs Up-

hear the sound, For soon no more the wild boar Will
on the ground,

ra- vish trav'llers on their way.

2. Against the bare black forest trees,
    The hunting coats are bright and gay:
  With loping stride and panting breath
    The blood-hounds bring their beasts to bay.
  All the merry woods are glad
    To hear the sound,
  Of the horses pounding hoofs
    Upon the ground,
  For soon no more
    The wild boar
  Will assail travellers on their way.

3. Come, come, mine host pile high the fire!
    Let's see the flames and shadows play,
  For while it burns the hunt returns –
    Out in the court the horses neigh.
  (Chorus)

4. With utmost care the grooms attend
    In stable sweet with new-spread hay,
  And round the board both king and knight
    Their lordly manners now display.
  (Chorus)

26. Alleluia

A round in three parts

This nativity round, by virtue of its $^{12}/_4$ tempo, builds up into an experience of musical circling. Botticelli's *Mystic Nativity* shows the angelic host similarly circling over the stable and the events below.

27. The Song of Christmas Day

A round in four parts

The joy of the shepherds after the Nativity has been a contagious element in carols all over the world. In that same spirit, Brien Masters wrote this piece after a visit to see Raphael's *Bridgewater Madonna* in the National Gallery of Scotland.

An- gels are throng-ing on their way; Shep-herds are danc-ing;

Hear their round-e-lay Of love for the babe who lies in the hay.

28. New Year

A round in four parts

This round by Walter Braithwaite is great fun to sing at New Year celebrations. Gentle accentuation on the notes shown will help give the effect of peals of bells. The words are by Eileen Hutchins.

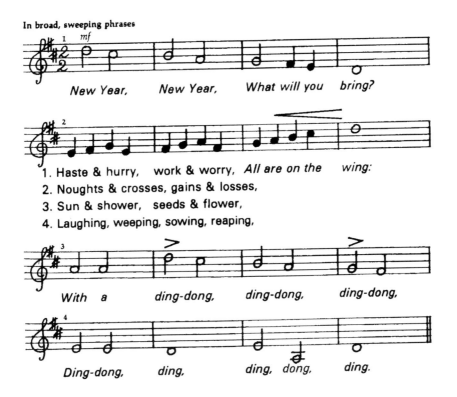

In broad, sweeping phrases

New Year, New Year, What will you bring?

1. Haste & hurry, work & worry, *All are on the* wing:
2. Noughts & crosses, gains & losses,
3. Sun & shower, seeds & flower,
4. Laughing, weeping, sowing, reaping,

With a ding-dong, ding-dong, ding-dong,

Ding-dong, ding, ding, dong, ding.

29. Where is John?

A round in three parts

Apart from being a good vocal rollick, the long-held top note of the third line gives a fine example of a tonic pedal. This is beautifully offset by the cantering rhythm of the first two lines.

Where is John? The old red hen has left her pen.

Where is John? The cows are in the corn a-gain, O

John ——————————————————————————.

30. To Wander is the Miller's Joy

A song by Schubert

This piece begins Schubert's song cycle 'Die schöne Müllerin' of 1823–1824. The suggested recorder asides and introduction are intended to give an experience of Schubert's unfailing sense of proportion in his music.

1. To wan-der is the mil- ler's joy To wan- der

2. The water 'twas that taught us this, the water, *(repeat)*
   That day or night no rest has known,
   And still must wander on and on,
   The water, the water ...

3. We learn it from the mill-wheels too, the mill-wheels, *(repeat)*
   They turn all day with right good will
   And love not to be standing still,
   The mill-wheels, ...

4. The millstones, too, for all their weight, the millstones, *(repeat)*
   They dance along in merry mood
   And would go quicker if they could,
   The millstones, ...

5. To wander is my only joy, to wander, *(repeat)*
   O master mine and mistress dear,
   Bid me no longer tarry here,
   But wander, and wander,
   But wander, and wander.

31. Love is Come Again

The third note of this song gives the melody a unique uplift as if major is about to emerge from minor. In this way it evokes spring emerging from winter: the first aconites and snowdrops, hazel catkins and greening larches. The similarly uplifting words are by J.M.C. Crumm.

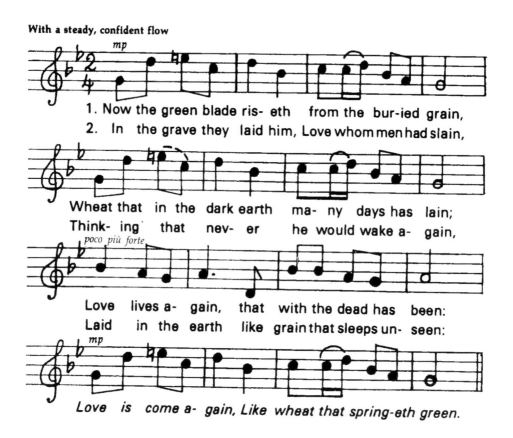

With a steady, confident flow

1. Now the green blade ris- eth   from the bur-ied grain,
2. In the grave they laid him, Love whom men had slain,

Wheat that in the dark earth ma- ny days has lain;
Think- ing that nev- er he would wake a- gain,

Love lives a- gain, that with the dead has been:
Laid in the earth like grain that sleeps un- seen:

Love is come a- gain, Like wheat that spring-eth green.

3. Forth he came at Easter, like the risen grain,
   He that for three days in the grave had lain,
   Quick from the dead my risen Lord is seen:
   Love is come again, …

4. When our hearts are wintry, grieving, or in pain,
   Thy touch can call us back to life again,
   Fields of our hearts that dead and bare have been:
   Love is come again, …

32. A Sea Bird to her Chicks

A Gaelic song

This charming song seems to breathe a lively spring air across the wings of the gulls and terns at nesting time, the elements mingling in a symphony of regeneration. The words in the *italic* transliteration are pronounced as familiar English ones.

33. Tomorrow Shall be my Dancing Day

A joyous Easter song that interweaves religion and dance. Verses from the 1833 version have been added to, in order to strengthen the elements of resurrection in the story.

3. Before Pilate the Jews me brought,
   Where Barabbas had deliverance;
   They scourgèd me and set me at nought,
   Judged me to die to lead the dance:
   Sing O my love…

4. Then on the cross hangèd I was,
   Where a spear to my heart did glance;
   There issued forth both water and blood,
   To call my true love to my dance:
   Sing O my love…

5. And as the sun, in chariot gold,
   Was dulled, like knight unhorsed by lance,
   The earth did quake, the rocks were rent
   Beneath the trembling of the dance.
   Sing O my love…

6. Then down to hell I took my way
   For my true love's deliverance,
   And rose again on the third day,
   Up to my true love and to dance:
   Sing O my love…

7. With spices rare they came at morn
   But stood amazed, as in a trance,
   When they beheld the stone rolled back,
   To set me free to lead the dance.
   Sing O my love…

8. In raiment white my angel stood --
   Like lightning was his countenance --
   Whereat the keepers shook with fear,
   Dead to my true love and the dance.
   Sing O my love…

9. Then in the garden I appeared
   My love's new dawning to enhance;
   In upper room, on sandy shore
   I led the gathering Easter dance.
   Sing O my love…

10. Then up to heaven I did ascend,
    Where now I dwell in sure substance
    On the right hand of God, that man
    May come unto the general dance:
    Sing O my love…

34. Kookaburra

An Australian round in four parts

The eucalyptus, or 'gum-tree' referred to in this song, survives incredible periods of drought in the Australian bush. It gives character to the landscape and offers sustenance to insects, birds and the koala bear, which clings to the smooth trunk, munching and sleeping.

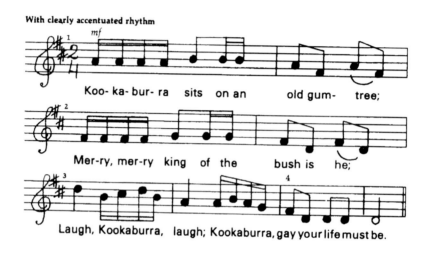

35. Bells Ring, Rise and Sing

A Finnish melody; words by Catherine van Alphen.

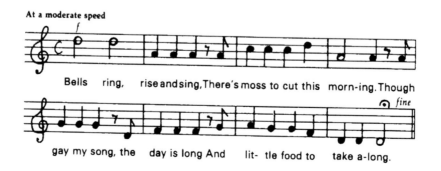

48

gay my song, the   day is long And   lit- tle food to   take a-long.

legato

mp

As-pens call me   hith- er, thith-er, Lin-den trees are   sooth-ing,

DC al fine

Brooms I make from bir-ken bran-ches   at   the dusk of   eve- ning.

36. O Soldier, Soldier, Won't You Marry Me?

A traditional song that children will enjoy acting out.

Briskly

mp

"O   soldier,   soldier, won't you marry me, With your musket, fife and drum?" "Oh

fine

mf

no, sweet maid, I   cannot marry thee, For I   have no 1. coat to put on!"   Then
                                                 2. hat 3. gloves 4. boots
                      5. For I   have a   wife of my own!"

up she went to her grandfather's chest And got him a 1. coat Of the   very,   very best, She
                                       2. hat
                           some 3. gloves 4. boots

got him a 1. coat Of the very,   very   best, And the   soldier   put   it   on.
              2. hat
        some 3. gloves 4. boots   them

37. I Bind Unto Myself Today

St Patrick's Hymn

St Patrick's faith, a spiritual rock upon which so many have found sure ground, is boldly stated here both in the translation of his words and in the old Irish melody. This hymn brings to light the enormous contribution Celtic Christianity has made to the cultural life of Europe.

sun's life- giv- ing ray, The white- ness of the
watch, his might to stay, His ear to heark- en

moon at ev'n, The flash- ing of the light- ning
to my need. The wis- dom of my God to

free, The whirl- ing wind's tem- pes-tuous shocks, The
teach, His hand to guide, his shield to ward; The

sta- ble earth, and deep salt sea, A-
word of God to give me speech, His

-round the old e- ter- nal rocks.
heav'n- ly host to be my guard.

38. In the Red of Evening

Schubert is known to have had an intimate connection with the mood of nature at sunset. This is expressed potently in this *Lied*, 'Am Abendrot', which has been slightly adapted here.

Tenderly and with sustained tone

Oh how fair this world of thine, Fa-ther, in the sun-set
Bask-ing in thy gaze di-vine, Ev-en dust to beau-ty

burn- ing,
turn- ing When the clouds are chang'd to shades of rose

and my west- ern win-dow glows. Gone is weep- ing

fled is sor- row, Now I feel thy pre- sence near. Then se-

-rene will dawn to- mor-row, Pa-ra- dise is here be- low,

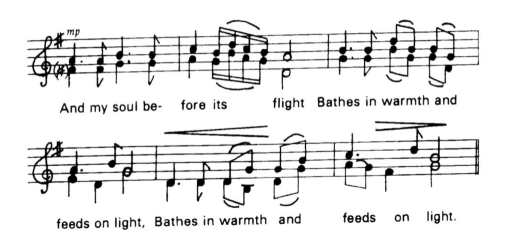

And my soul be- fore its flight Bathes in warmth and feeds on light, Bathes in warmth and feeds on light.

39. We've Ploughed our Land

A clapping round in three or four parts

This round by Tom Scratchley is enjoyable and relaxing when performed in four parts. The fourth line is clapped only, or played with a percussion instrument.

Quickly, but not skating over the notes

We've plough'd our land, we've sown our seed, we've made all neat and gay,

So take a bit and leave a bit, a- way birds, a- way.

Shoo ah oh shoo ah shoo oh.

CLAP

40. For All the Saints

Vaughan Williams

Vaughan Williams (1872–1958) wrote the music 'Sine Nomine' especially for this hymn.

41. Alleluia for All Things

Cecil Harwood particularly admired the melody from the previous song, and these words accompany it perfectly, not only in the culminating 'Alleluia', but in its magnanimous gesture towards creation. An associate of Vaughan Williams, C.S. Lewis and Owen Barfield, Harwood was one of the pioneers of the Waldorf movement in the English-speaking world.

1. Of all created things, of earth and sky,
   Of God and Man, things lowly and things high,
   We sing this day with thankful heart and say,
   Alleluia, alleluia.

2. Of light and darkness and colours seven
   Stretching their rain-bow bridge from earth to heaven,
   We sing this day…

3. Of sun and moon, the lamps of night and day,
   Stars and planets sounding on their way,
   We sing this day…

4. Of times and seasons, evening and fresh morn,
   Of birth and death, green blade and golden corn,

5. Of all that lives and moves, the winds ablow,
   Fire and old ocean's never-resting flow,

6. Of earth and from earth's darkness springing free
   The flowers outspread, the heavenward reaching tree,

7. Of creatures all, the eagle in his flight,
   The patient ox, the lion that trusts his might,

8. Of Man, with hand outstretched for service high,
   Courage at heart, truth in his steadfast eye,

9. Of angels and archangels, spirits clear,
   Warders of souls and watchers of the year

10. Of God made Man, and through Man sacrificed,
    Of Man through love made God, Adam made Christ,

42. Iduna

Michael Wilson, whose work with Goethe's theory of colour has become widely known, wrote the melody for this song. Formerly an outstanding violinist, he often wrote melodies that could be sung in almost any circumstance. 'Iduna' was written for a school production of a Norse play about a guardian of precious stolen apples. The words are by Eileen Hutchins.

43. Bugles Gaily Call Us

A round in four parts

The brightness of the bugle tone finds musical expression in the fanfare-like phrase which sets this round in motion.

44. Clouds of Rain

A round in four parts

Whitsuntide is usually a concept for the older child, but the primary teacher may not wish to let it go unnoticed in younger years. This round incorporates a few simple images that can be built upon at a later date.

45. Glory to Thee, my God, this Night

A canon in eight parts

One of the fathers of the English Renaissance style, Thomas Tallis composed this famous canon around 1561 for Psalm 67. These words, and those of Thomas Ken's 'Awake my soul, and with the sun' have accompanied millions of people as they crossed the threshold of sleep ever since.

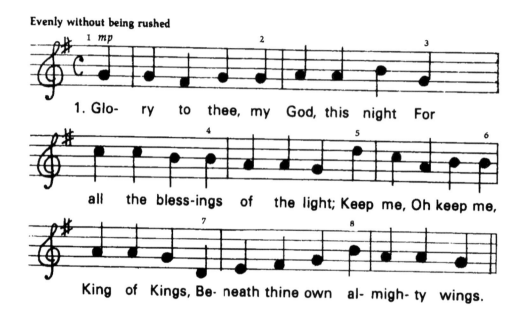

2. Oh may my soul on thee repose,
And with sweet sleep mine eyelids close,
Sleep that may me more vig'rous make
To serve my God when I awake.

3. Praise God, from whom all blessings flow;
Praise him, all creatures here below;
Praise him above, ye heavenly host;
Praise Father, Son, and Holy Ghost.

Class 5

From Age 10

46. Life from Dead Furrow

A Danish harvest song

This robust Danish folk tune associated with harvest has all the character of a jubilant dance rhythm.

Allegro *mf*

1. Life from dead fur- row, by plough-share once rif- ted;
High on the corn- rick, the ripe grain is lif- ted;

Sharpen'd scythes and swishing swathes, the har-vest time now starts;
Jogg-ling on the wa- gon: ti- red limbs but sing-ing hearts.

mp

Sun of the sum-mer's height, Brings us strength for win-ter's plight;

f

Loaves are bak- ing; Mer- ry mak- ing; Join the har-vest song.

2. So will be garnered the harvest of ages;
   Present, past, and future, whether bringing love or strife;
   Thought, word and action; both monarch and pages;
   All the little things that fill the round of daily life.
   Sun of the summer's height…

47. When Autumn Mists Gather

A canon in three parts

The virtual imperceptibility of the 2/4 bars is remarkable in this piece even as it is sung by a single voice. As a canon, the timelessness of the music is even more pronounced.

48. Bhajan

The traditional manner of singing a Gujarati Bhajan is to start slowly, repeat faster, repeat even faster again, and then to finally slow down the fourth time. A drum and Indian cymbals can be added as time keepers. The first of each set of sixteen notes should be emphasised strongly, then the dynamics can diminish as the beat 'evaporates'.

Translation:
O Lord, your name I hear in every place,
In the sky, breeze and forest;
In the garden and at the 'khal-khal' sound of the stream,
I hear your song.

49. Hail Light of Lights

Sanskrit

This ancient Sanskrit chant is an invocation to the light of lights.

50. The Fire of Ash Twigs

This song dwells on the remarkable combustibility of ash, even when green. Both words and music originate from the work of Margaret Bennell, founder of Wynstones School and Hawkwood College.

Jo-seph with his lan-tern went out in- to the night;

Jo-seph brought in branch-es, but none could he light.

On-ly the green ash twigs Jo-seph did not try: "How

can I kin-dle sap wood if I can-not kin-dle dry?"

"Try the ash twigs, Jo-seph, Green though they are. " The

ash twigs kin-dled like a leap- ing star. The

ash twigs kin-dled like a glow- ing sun.

"Now a sap of sun- light In the ash shall run;

O-ther trees shall kin-dle on-ly when dead, But ash shall kin-dle green or dry," the young child said.

51. Sanctus

A round in five parts

The superbly lyrical quality of sacred Renaissance music finds simple expression in this round attributed to Pope Clemens.

Moderato expressivo

Sanct————us, sanct————us, sanct————us, sanct————us, sanct————us.

52. O Holy Night

A round in four parts

Even a beginner on the cello can play this ostinato simply by using the open C and G strings an octave below the notes given.

CELLOS OR MEN'S VOICES (OPTIONAL)

53. Three Kings Come Star-led Riding

A round in three parts

This round is a perfect way to introduce the concept of counterpoint to younger children. Careful counting will help to carry the beautiful flow of discord and resolution forward.

Con moto non troppo

Three kings come star-led rid- ing, From distant lands full of mys- ter-

-y old; To seek, to seek out a king is their in- tent

——, a king of won- der un- told; They come to the child of

Mary mild, And give him their myrrh, frankin-cense and gold.

54. Come All Ye Jolly Shanty Boys

A Canadian lumbering song

Logging or lumbering, common in all tundra regions, is a treacherous as well as exciting task. Skidders and swampers get the logs down river using cant-hooks to lever and grip them and jam-pikes to free them when they dam the river. This song goes wonderfully with practical woodworking tasks.

2. The choppers and the sawyers, they lay the timber low
   The skidders and the swampers, they holler to and fro.
   And then there come the loaders, before the break of day,
   Come load up the teams, boys, and to the woods away.

3. The broken ice is floating, and sunny is the sky,
   Three hundred big and strong men, are ready, wet or dry.
   With cant hooks and with jam pikes, these noble men do go
   And risk their lives each springtime, on some big stream you know.

55. Blow the Wind Southerly

A Northumbrian song

This exceptionally beautiful Northumbrian folk song was often used as an unaccompanied encore by the world famous contralto, Kathleen Ferrier. Its calming melody will bring a reflective peace to the classroom.

2. Blow the wind southerly, southerly, southerly,
Blow bonny breeze o'er the bonny sea.
Blow the winds southerly, southerly, southerly,
Blow bonny breeze, my lover to me.
Is it not sweet to hear the breeze singing,
As lightly it comes o'er the deep rolling sea?
But sweeter and dearer by far when 'tis bringing
The bark of my true love in safety to me.

56. Farewell Night

These Easter verses, written for this Highland melody, draw attention to the great imaginative wealth of Gaelic culture. More of Alexander Carmichael's extensive research into Gaelic consciousness is published by Floris Books in the *Carmina Gadelica*.

Andante

1. Fare- well night with mists o'ershrouded, Fare- well star and twi-light gloom; Wel-come sun-shine un- be-cloud-ed; Win- ter make for May- day room! *Heav'n and earth,* Isle and o- cean, Frith and firth, *Sing for mirth.*

2. Gold bright sun of spring's new morning
   Rising o'er the crests of hills,
   Dance now in thy robes of splendour
   While the Easter clarion trills. *(Chorus)*

3. Earth's fair mantle green and glistening,
   Soften'd by the April show'rs
   Burgeon forth to greet Life's Hero
   Yield your ransomed scent and flow'rs. *(Chorus)*

57. Easter Day

Musically, this Easter song is exceptional in two ways: first, its opening phrases burst ecstatically into the upper octave; and second, the melody is in the Phrygian mode rather than in C major.

Allegro giocoso

1. The world it-self keeps Eas-ter Day, & Eas-ter larks are sing-ing; And Eas-ter flow'rs are blooming gay, And Eas-ter buds are springing; Al-le-lu-ia, al-le-lu-ia: The Lord of all things lives a-new, And all his works are ris-ing too, *In no-va ju-ven-tu-te.*

2. There stood three Marys by the tomb,
   On Easter morning early;
   When day had scarcely chas'd the gloom,
   And dew was white and pearly:
   Alleluia, alleluia:
   With loving but with erring mind,
   They came the Prince of Life to find,
   Cum pia servitute.

3. But earlier still the angel sped,
   His news of comfort giving:
   And "Why," he said, "among the dead
   Thus seek ye for the living?"
   Alleluia, alleluia:
   "Go, tell them all, and make them blest,
   Tell Peter first, and then the rest,"
   Mandatum hoc secute.

58. Ye Banks and Braes o' Bonny Doon

This song refers to the picturesque region of south-west Scotland associated with Robert Burns. The Doon Valley is also famed for its bridge, which is mentioned in 'Tam o' Shanter'.

Andantino

1. Ye banks and braes o' bon-ny Doon, How can ye bloom sae fresh and fair! How can ye chaunt ye lit- tle birds, and I sae wea- ry fu' o' care! Ye'll break my heart, ye warb-ling birds that war- ble on the flow'r-y thorn, Ye 'mind me o' de-par- ted joys, de-par- ted ne-ver to re-turn.

59. St Francis' Hymn

Martin Shaw longed to set Matthew Arnold's version of St Francis' testimony of life in this way, using a Parisian tone as the starting point. The exact length of the breves |O| should be taken only as an approximation – just enough for the relevant words to be chanted at a measured speed.

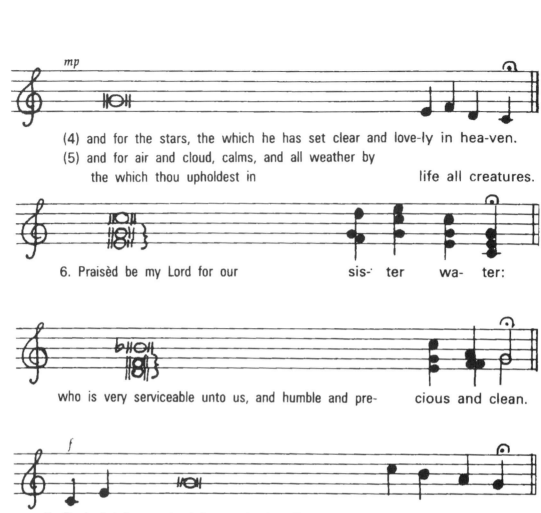

(4) and for the stars, the which he has set clear and love-ly in hea-ven.
(5) and for air and cloud, calms, and all weather by
the which thou upholdest in life all creatures.

6. Praisèd be my Lord for our sis- ter wa- ter:

who is very serviceable unto us, and humble and pre- cious and clean.

7. Prais-èd be my Lord for our brother fire,
through whom thou givest us light in the dark-ness:

8. Prais-èd be my Lord for our mother the earth,
the which doth sustain us and keep us;

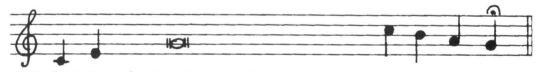

(7) and he is bright and pleasant and very migh-ty and strong.
(8) and bringeth forth divers fruit, and flowers of many co-lours, and grass.

9. Praisèd be my Lord
for all those who   for his love's sake; and who endure
pardon one another   weakness and tri- bu- la- tion.

10. Blessèd are they who
peaceably shall endure: For thou, O most
Highest, shalt give them a crown.

11. Prais-èd be my Lord for our sister the death   of the bo- dy:

blessed are they who are found walking by the most   ho- ly will.

12. Praise ye   and bless ye the Lord and give   thanks un- to him:

and serve him with   great hu-mi- li- ty. Al- le- lu- ia, al- le- lu- ia!

ome Follow

A round in three parts

To be sung in the best tradition of English rounds – vigorously and tunefully.

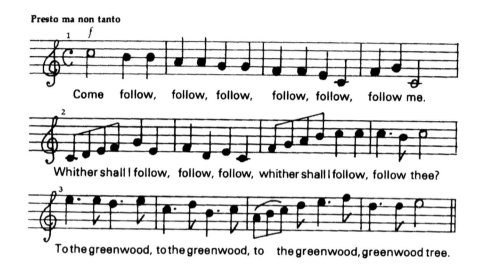

61. Che Farò Senza Euridice?

An Italian song from Gluck's *Orfeo*

This aria comes at one of the most poignant moments in operatic history – as Orpheus loses Eurydice on his return from the netherworld. Gluck's masterpiece rises to the occasion in such a way that the melody, here abridged to A-B-A form, can be savoured even without accompaniment.

-drò che fa- rò sen- za il mi- o

ben do- ve an- drò sen- za il mi- o

ben? Eur-i- di- ce Eur-i- di- ce O

Di- o ri- spon- di ri- spon———

———di; io son pu- re il tu-o fe- de- le son

pu- re il tu-o fe- de- le il tu-o fe- de- le.

62. Good Friends When Gathered Together

A round in four parts

Despite its minor key, this short round fizzes with the good-natured feeling that arises when people gather together. Some emphasis should be given to the recurring syncopation (♪♪).

Good friends when gather'd to-gether, Sing for the joy of sing-ing;

No mat- ter what the weather; Good friends are happy to-gether.

63. On the Hills the John-Fires Burn

A round in six parts

In many northern European countries, particularly Estonia and Latvia, the summer solstice festivities centre around all-night midsummer fires.

On the hills the John-fires burn; Flickering flames now leap and turn;

Hand in hand we all ad-vance To seek the warmth & join the dance; Rise,

too, my soul, en- dur-ing light, And, flame-like, burn for e- ver bright.

64. Migildi Magildi

A Welsh folk song

Nonsense, riddle, or double Dutch? Songs in this vein are found in more than one folk-song tradition, in one form or another.

2. When the winter's bright in May-time, *Migildi...*
   When the stars shine in the day-time, *Migildi...*
   When from earth to heaven takes seconds, *Migildi...*
   O then I'll wake when David beckons. *Migildi...*

65. Glorious Apollo

A part song by Samuel Webbe

This piece became the traditional opening song for the first ever Glee Club, founded in London in 1790. Its members would gather together for an evening's singing of glees (or part-songs) and general jollity.

While we our- selves such a struc-ture might raise,

Thus then com- bin- ing, Hands & hearts join- ing

Sing we in har- mo-ny A- pol- lo's praise.

66. Sleep, Refreshing

A canon in three parts

Attributed to Mozart, this is strictly a musical canon and not a round, i.e. the second part enters before the first phrase is complete. A natural-sounding melody such as this is notoriously hard to create in this kind of composition.

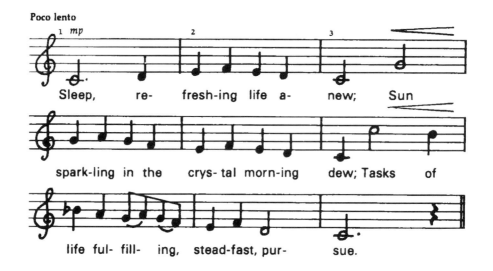

67. Greensleeves

This immortal melody springs from the very soil of English folk music. In *Sir John in Love*, Vaughan Williams brought this most popular of English melodies together with a most popular of Shakespearean characters, Falstaff. It is worth making an effort to get the accidentals exact.

cast me off dis-cour-teous-ly, And I have lov- éd

you so long, de- light- ing in your com- pa- ny.

piu forte

Green-sleeves was all my joy, Green- sleeves was

my de-light, Greensleeves was my heart of gold, And

LAST TIME

who but my la- dy Green-sleeves. | Green-sleeves.

2. I have been ready at your hand
   To grant whatever you would crave,
   I have both wagèd life and land,
   Your love and goodwill for to have,
   Greensleeves was all my joy...

3. I bought three kerchers to thy head,
   That were wrought fine and gallantly,
   I kept thee both at board and bed,
   Which cost my purse well favour'dly.
   Greensleeves...

4. Well I will pray to God on high
   That thou my constancy mayst see,
   And that yet once before I die
   Thou wilt vouchsafe to love me.
   Greensleeves...

Class 6

From Age 11

68. Michaelmas Time

A festive song

Michael Rose, who wrote this song, is a founder teacher at the York Rudolf Steiner School.

2. Michaelmas time! Michaelmas time!
   Time is bending over the scales.
   Over the bread, over the wine,
   The ploughman bows his head at the rail.
   He turns his thoughts towards the flame,
   Raises his eyes to the thanksgiven grain;
   Stars, like spears, gleam over the tower
   Of the House of God in Michaël's hour.

3. Michaelmas time! Michaelmas time!
   Time is changing the guard of the world.
   Deep in his heart, dauntless in mind,
   The ploughman guards against time growing old.
   He stands and studies the star-patterned sky,
   Fixes each spark in his wishing-well eyes:
   Stars, like seeds, strewn over the land
   And under the plough by Michaël's hand.

69. Sunrise is Flaming

A round in three parts

Round writing, often simply for singing with friends, was a popular pastime among classical composers. This one was written by Luigi Cherubini (1760–1842), a composer whom Beethoven particularly admired.

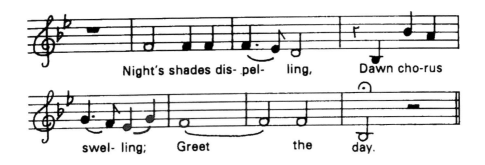

Night's shades dis- pel- ling, Dawn cho-rus
swel- ling; Greet the day.

70. Deo Gratias

A round in four parts

This translation captures the original essence of the angel's message to the shepherds in St Luke's Gospel.

Moderato cantabile

De- o, De- o gra- ti- as
To all men of good will; There
shall be peace on earth for them; A—
—men, A———————men.

71. The Mermaid

A popular example of sea-songs that recall the empire-building days, when the merchant navy played an important economic role in many European nations.

Allegro vivo

1. One   Fri-   day morn, when we   set   sail, And our
2. Then   up spoke the cap-   tain of our gallant ship, Who at

ship not far from   land,   We there did es- py   a
once did our per-il   see,   "I have mar-ried a wife   in

fair   pret-ty maid, With a comb and a   glass   in her
fair   London town, And this night she a   wi-   dow will

hand, her hand, her hand, With a comb and a   glass   in her
be, will be, will be, And this night she a   wi-   dow will

hand.   While the ra- ging seas   did   roar, And the
be".   For the

storm-y winds did blow, And we, jol-ly sailor boys, were

up, up a- loft, And the land lub-bers ly- ing down be-

-low, be-low, be-low, And the landsmen were all down be- low.

3. And then up spoke the little cabin boy,
   And a fair hair'd boy was he;
   "I've a father and mother in fair Portsmouth town,
   And this night they will weep for me, for me, for me,
   And this night they will weep for me. *For the…*

4. Then three times round went our gallant ship,
   And three times round went she;
   For the want of a lifeboat they both went down,
   As she sunk to the bottom of the sea, the sea, the sea,
   As she sunk to the bottom of the sea. *For the…*

72. Make We Merry

The melody appears in the lower part of this tune, which is derived from a thirteenth-century dance called the 'Estampie'. This version can be supported by percussion or sung unaccompanied, as many dances in this tradition were.

73. Ring Out, Wild Bells

Alfred, Lord Tennyson (1809–1892)

Bring forth the New Year with this vibrant song of renewal and hope. Tennyson's sure-handed mastery of poetic form is exemplified here in his taking up of a familiar metre but with the less familiar rhyming pattern a-b-b-a.

3. Ring out a slowly dying cause,
    And ancient forms of party strife;
    Ring in the nobler modes of life,
With sweeter manners, purer laws.

4. Ring out false pride in place and blood,
    The civic slander and the spite;
    Ring in the love of truth and right,
    Ring in the common love of good.

5. Ring out old shapes of fould disease;
    Ring out the narrowing lust of gold;
    Ring out the thousand wars of old,
Ring in the thousand years of peace.

6. Ring in the valiant man and free,
    The larger heart, the kindlier hand;
    Ring out the darkness of the land,
    Ring in the Christ that is to be.

74. Juvivalera

A classic, cheery mountain song, perfect for a hike in the Black Forest in southern Germany.

2. Not long doth the sun in his blue tent remain,
   He flames o'er the ocean, he rolls o'er the plain;
   The sea-wave grows weary of lapping the shore,
   And the blasts of the tempests, how loudly they roar.
   Juvivalera…

3. The bird on the white cloud is hurried along,
   Afar doth it warble its home-loving song;
   So speeds the young wand'rer through forest and fell,
   Since his mother earth hasteth, he hasteth as well.
   Juvivalera…

75. How Cool Blows the Breeze

From Weber's *Der Freischütz*

Alongside a spate of settings of Goethe's *Faust, Der Freischütz* is a prime example of the then obsession with the (often grotesque) supernatural. This huntsman's chorus alternately illustrates the very tangible experience of the striking German forests.

Molto vivace

1. How cool blows the breeze in the deep fo-rest glade Where
   In gol- den and rus- set they dance over all And

leaves whisper soft-ly in sun-shine and shade. A- bove the wide
gai- ly they carpet the ground where they fall.

branch-es and up to the skies. We see tow'ring moun-tains be-

-fore us a- rise, And then like the swal-lows that swift-ly de-

part, We haste to the hills with a joy- ful heart.

2. Oh, sweet is the spell of the chill misty morn,
   The tall scented pines and the dew-studded dawn,
   And fresh is the stream as it sparkles so clear,
   What joy to be walking when autumn is here!
   Above the wide branches…

76. When Winter Skies

A round in three parts by Carl Loewe

Carl Loewe (1796–1869), who composed this slightly adapted three-part song, was famed for his ballads. He had an exceptional voice and gave magnificent recitals throughout Europe.

Moderato

a piacere

1. When win- ter skies are o- ver-cast & days are dark and
2. So when the storms of life grow dark, with need and
Threat'ning

1. New hope a-ris- es in my heart, New hope a-ris- es
2. That light of hope within my heart, That light of hope with-

drear,
pain,

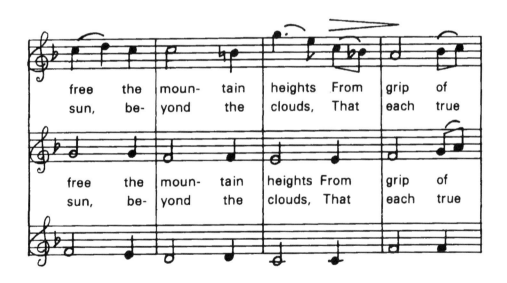

97

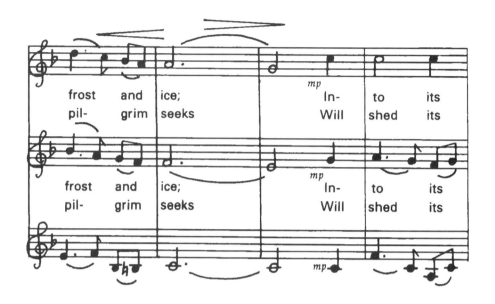

frost and ice; In- to its
pil- grim seeks Will shed its

frost and ice; In- to its
pil- grim seeks Will shed its

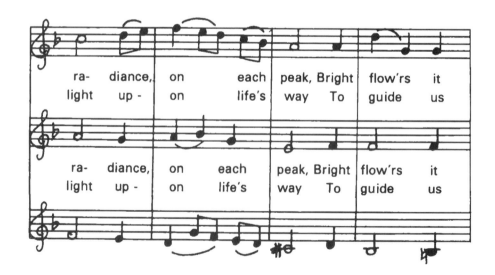

ra- diance, on each peak, Bright flow'rs it
light up - on life's way To guide us

ra- diance, on each peak, Bright flow'rs it
light up - on life's way To guide us

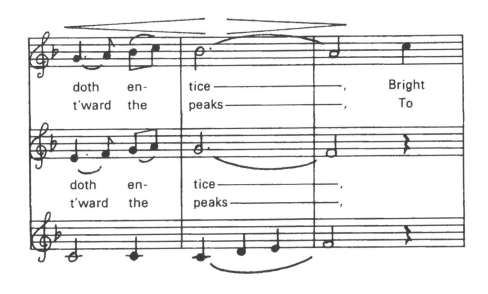

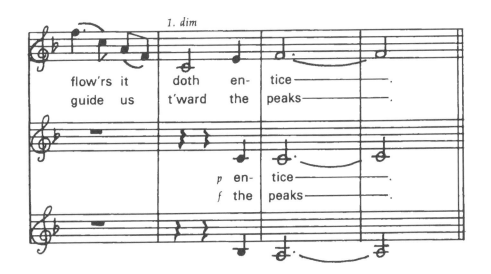

77. Storming, Roaring, Wintry Winds

A round in three parts by Joseph Haydn

This is a particularly vigorous round of Haydn's. The words were written especially to draw out the varied features of the music.

Allegro ben marcato

1. Storming, roaring, wint- ry winds are pier- cing cold;

2. Lashing, slashing i- cy cold, they freeze your

3. Flaring and flaming. Then what care we how the wintry twigs smite against the

bellowing, blustering they make all the boughs bend,

nose red raw; so stoke up the fire and set it

window pane: inside we are hap- py while out- side it's

78. Pange Lingua

Or, 'Sing my Tongue the Glorious Battle'

In the Middle Ages, saintly and sacred relics were among the most treasured possessions of the monasteries. This chant, styled to resemble early notation, is associated with the legend of a fragment of the True Cross held at Poitiers in France. The first verse is given in traditional Latin and English, and a further verse has been added to facilitate closer study of the legend.

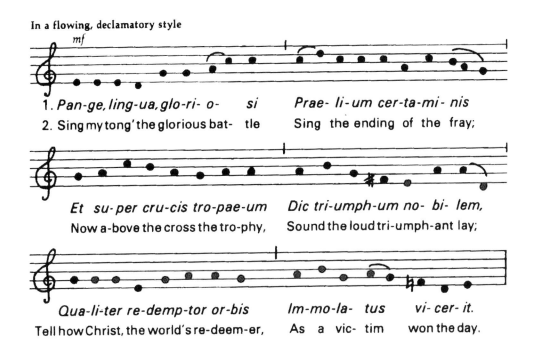

In a flowing, declamatory style

mf

1. *Pan-ge, ling-ua, glo-ri- o-*   *si*   *Prae- li- um cer-ta-mi- nis*
2. Sing my tong' the glorious bat- tle   Sing the ending of the fray;

Et su- per cru-cis tro-pae-um   *Dic tri-umph-um no- bi- lem,*

Now a-bove the cross the tro-phy,   Sound the loud tri-umph-ant lay;

Qua-li-ter re-demp-tor or-bis   *Im-mo-la- tus*   *vi- cer- it.*

Tell how Christ, the world's re-deem-er,   As a vic- tim   won the day.

3. Noble Cross on Calv'ry lifted;
   From thy dead wood new life streams;
   Hope eternal rising ever,
   New-born sun from darkness gleams;
   Death's cold mouth acclaims the victor:
   Easter Lord the world redeems.

4. *Pange, lingua, gloriosi*
   (As verse 1, ad lib)

79. Under the Leaves of Life

This is an example of some of the finest devotional folk poetry in existence.

3. "We're seeking for no leaves, Thomas,
   But for a friend of thine;
   We're seeking for sweet Jesus Christ,
   To be our guide and thine."

4. "Go you down, go you down to yonder town,
   And sit in the gallery;
   And there you'll find sweet Jesus Christ,
   Nailed to a big yew-tree."

5. "Dear mother, dear mother, you must take John,
   All for to be your son,
   And he will comfort you sometimes,
   Mother, as I have done."

6. "O come, thou, John Evangelist,
   Thou'rt welcome unto me,
   But more welcome than my own dear son,
   That I nursed upon my knee."

7. The he laid his head on his right shoulder,
   Seeing death it struck him nigh:
   "The Holy Ghost be with your soul;
   I die, mother dear, I die."

8. Oh the rose, the rose, the gentle rose,
   And the fennel that grows so green!
   God give us grace in ev'ry place,
   To pray for our King and Queen.

80. When Daffodils on Fields of Green

A round in four parts

This beautiful round is ascribed to Orlando di Lasso (1532–1594), one of the geniuses of Renaissance music. Although it can be experienced as a progression of harmonies, this round belongs to an era when music was conceived in polyphonic, simultaneous melodies.

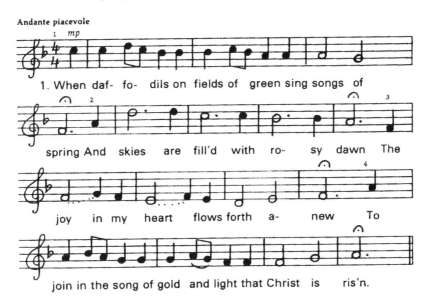

Andante piacevole

1. When daf- fo- dils on fields of green sing songs of spring And skies are fill'd with ro- sy dawn The joy in my heart flows forth a- new To join in the song of gold and light that Christ is ris'n.

2. And thus it was on Easter morn the Marys came
   With hearts weigh'd down and tears of love,
   They made their way through the garden dew.
   The light of their life had set in depths of darkest night.

3. "Oh who will roll away the stone?" in grief they cried,
   For deaf were they to lark and thrush,
   As near the sepulchre they came
   Wherein the body of the Lord was laid to rest.

4. But marvel rare! The stone roll'd back with mighty quake;
   Upon it sat the youth from heav'n,
   As white as snow was the robe he wore,
   Like lightning was his countenance, his forehead flame.

5. With finger rais'd to heav'n he spake: "He is not here."
   Whereat the sorrow from their hearts
   Like stone from the tomb was roll'd away;
   "To Galilee, O fairest land, we make our way."

81. Why with Bulrush Mock Him?

An Easter passion, this low mixolydian Scottish folk tune was first used in 1924. Unlike the northern European artists who preferred to present the harshness of the events at Golgotha, G.R. Woodward merely sought to emphasise the incredulity felt by Jesus' followers.

3. Why unknown, the world's Redeemer?
   Bound, scourged by harsh blasphemer?
   Helpless He – of all, supremer?
   Bound and scourged by harsh blasphemer?
   Why unknown the world's Redeemer?

4. Easter sun will brim day's dawning;
   Joy will follow night of mourning;
   Vict'ry conquer hell's gate yawning;
   Joy will follow night of mourning;
   Easter sun will brim day's dawning.

82. The Streams in the Mountains

A round in three parts

When the snow melts off the lower Alpine shoulders, animals are taken up to graze in the higher pastures for a new season. This is a German song used in some of the traditional festivities common to all regions of the Alps at this time of year.

The streams in the mountains Are tumb-ling like fountains;

With yo- d'ling in the val-ley, And cow- bells in spring.

Fa- la-la- la-la- la-la- la——, Fa- la-la- la-la- la-la- la.

83. While the Flames Leap Up

A round in three parts

The bars that start with a crotchet rest give this round a charming buoyancy.

84. Light Ever Gladsome

An Italian three-part folk hymn

The richness, mellowness, and serenity of the Italian landscape at eventide is here expressed in a simple but telling three-part melody. The dynamics of each verse should reflect the changing mood of the words.

85. The Lord my Pasture Shall Prepare

Psalm 23, set to music by Haydn

Addison's metrical version of Psalm 23 is here combined with a melody attributed to Haydn. The composer's masterly handling of the wide intervals, when matched by the singers, reaches the very peaks of classical melody.

1. The Lord my pasture shall prepare, And
2. When in the sultry glebe I faint, Or

feed me with a shepherd's care; His presence
on the thirsty mountain pant, To fertile

shall my wants supply, And guard me with a
vales and dewy meads My weary wand'ring

watchful eye; My noonday walks he shall at-
steps he leads, Where peaceful rivers, soft and

-tend, And all my midnight hours defend.
slow, Amid the verdant landscape flow.

3. Though in a bare and rugged way
   Through devious lonely wilds I stray,
   Thy bounty shall my pains beguile;
   The barren wilderness shall smile
   With sudden greens and herbage crowned.
   And streams shall murmur all around.

4. Though in the paths of death I tread,
   With gloomy horrors overspread,
   My steadfast heart shall fear no ill,
   For thou, O Lord, art with me still
   Thy friendly crook shall give me aid,
   And guide me through the dreadful shade.

86. Fie, Nay Prithee, John

A round in three parts by Henry Purcell

Through this musical telescope of a round, Purcell provides us a glimpse into seventeenth-century social life for the average man.

87. The Veil of Destiny is Drawn

From Mozart's *The Magic Flute*

In 1790, Mozart's folk opera *The Magic Flute* made its first impression on the Viennese and on the world. This is one of the trios sung by the three genii at a crucial moment in the story. Critics often view the story as mere pantomime, but this English version seeks to give expression to the deeper relevance of the story.

88. Anne de Bretagne

A French folk song

This song recounts how it was prophesied that Anne, Duchess of Brittany would become Queen of France, clogs 'n' all (*les sabots de bois*). Handed a sprig of verbena at the gates of Rennes, she was told that if it flowered she would become Queen. The story is here contained within five verses of two lines with an intervening refrain; the original form is as follows:

    Verse 1: Line 1, repeat, line 2, chorus;
    Verse 2: Line 2, repeat, line 3, chorus, and so on.

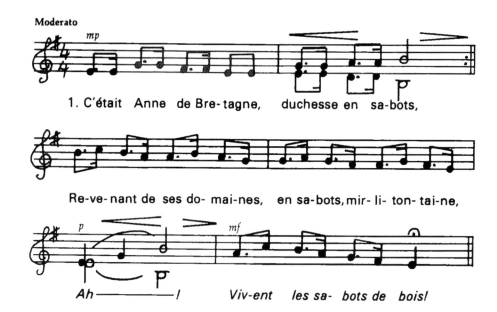

2. Entourée de chatelaines, avec ses sabots, (2)
   Voila, qu'aux portes de Rennes, en sabots
   mirlitontaine
     Ah! Vivent les sabots de bois!

3. L'ou vit trois beaux capitaines, avec ses sabots (2)
   Offiri a leur souveraine, en sabots
   mirlitontaine
     Ah! Vivent les sabots de bois!

4. Un joli pied de verveine, avec ses sabots (2)
   "S'il fleurit tu seras Reine" en sabots
   mirlitontaine
     Ah! Vivent les sabots de bois!

5. Elle a fleuri la verveine, avec ses sabots (2)
   Anne de France fut reine, en sabots
   mirlitontaine
     Ah! Vivent les sabots de bois!

89. Headstrong Horses on the Plain

A Hungarian canon in two, three, four or more parts

This bracing canon captures the longstanding tradition of excellent horsemanship among the tribes of Hungary. Depending on the class's musical abilities, this exciting canon can be performed simply in two parts (the second entering comfortably after one bar), or by adding in the extra parts overleaf.

Headstrong horses on the plain, Gal-lop-ing to- geth- er;

Matted manes and flashing eyes, Tails as light as feath-er;

Pound-ing bare-back side by side, Wave on wave like

surg-ing tide, O'er rock and spring-y heath- er;

Foaming mouths and fly-ing turf, Sweating hell-for-leather, Hi!

SEE OVER FOR SINGING IN PARTS

2-PART (AFTER 1/4 BAR)

Headstrong horses on the plain, Galloping to- geth-er; Matted manes and flashing eyes,

pp

Headstrong horses on the plain, Galloping to- geth-er; Matted manes and flashing

Tails as light as feath-er; Pound-ing bare-back side by side,

eyes, Tails as light as feather; bare-back side by side,

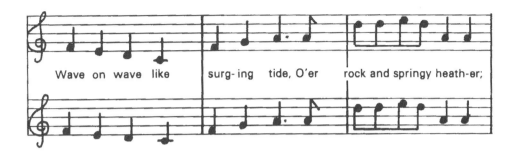

Wave on wave like surg-ing tide, O'er rock and springy heath-er;

Foaming mouths and fly-ing turf, Sweating hell-for-leather, Hi!

pp

fly-ing
Foaming mouths and turf, Sweating hell-for-leather, Hi!

3-PART   2   3   4-PART   2   3   4

AND SO ON TO EIGHT PARTS

115

Class 7

From Age 12

90. Michael Sea-Lord

A Celtic song

This unusual chant-like song expresses the Celts' strong connection with, and reliance upon, the supernatural world.

91. The Paths of Life are Steep

A round in three parts by Haydn

This round is ideally suited to older children as the chromatically widening intervals offer a real challenge to the singer.

92. Firmly on the Earth I Stand

A Michaelmas round in four parts with ostinato bass

This song is particularly atmospheric in a handsomely proportioned hall or stairway with good acoustics. In this case, the antiphonal effect can be enhanced by placing the groups some distance apart. Singers divide into two for the ostinato, the first group singing the part through once and then resting while the second group sings. Small notes in brackets below indicate the introduction of a new group.

93. Bubbling and Splashing

A round in three parts by Henry Purcell

John Blow made history when he gracefully made way for his gifted pupil, Henry Purcell (1659–1695), to replace him as organist at Westminster Abbey. This bustling song is a perfect example of Purcell's talents, and it paints a moral lesson too – a style that was in vogue in the late seventeenth century.

94. Ein Feste Burg

From Martin Luther's *Reformation*

An excellent accompaniment to a lesson on the history of the Reformation, this song expresses the staunch attitude widely held towards the Reformed faith. Martin Luther wholeheartedly embraced this cause in all aspects of his life – particularly in his vernacular verses and chorale melodies, which he wrote for the new Protestant congregations.

Ein fes- te Burg ist un- ser Gott, ein gu- te
Er hilft uns frei aus al- ler Not, die uns jetzt

Wehr und Waf- fen. Der alt bö- se
hat be- trof- fen.

Feind mit Ernst er's jetzt meint; gross Macht und viel List

sein grau-sam Rüst-ung ist, auf Erd' ist nicht seins glei- chen.

95. O God of Heaven, Hear my Praises

Lobgesang by Johann Sebastian Bach

The slurring within these musical phrases gives this melody a unique inner vigour – the unmistakable hallmark of the Lutheran Reformation. It is typical of the triumphant inner certainty expressed in many works of Johann Sebastian Bach (1685–1750).

1. O God of heaven, hear my praises;
   Deep in my soul Thy mighty strength I feel;
   Thy glorious work my heart upraises,
   All Thy creation doth Thy pow'r reveal;
   When Thou art by my side I fear not strife;
   In love to Thee I call, great Lord of Life.

2. In solitude to Thee inclining
   We can approach Thee in our daily pray'r;
   And where the stars of heav'n are shining
   In world expanses, Thou art surely there;
   Thy guiding hand led mankind in ages past,
   And Thou art with us now, unto the last.

96. Who Will Come to the Sea

A Dutch sea song

One of the supreme moments in Dutch history was its emancipation from the political yoke of Spain, thanks to the Dutch 'Sea beggars'. Their relentless fortitude and tenacity still epitomises the nation's connection with the ocean.

1. Who will come now with me to the sea?
2. Brave and strong, go we now to the sea! *Hold her fast now!*
3. Then we'll give three cheers for the sea!

Fresh blows the wind thro' furrows free.   You may
Rea-   dy to keep our country free.   With an
Men   of   Holland, shout with me!   For the

stay   on   shore with the   rest,
eye   on the sail as   we   haul, *Hold her fast   now!*
sea   makes   he- roes of   all,

Life   on   the   sea   is   still the   best!   He who
Glad-   ly   we   heed our country's call!   Upward
On-   ly   the   brave will heed her call!   In   a

fame   would find   does not   stay be-. hind,   No   he
turn   our   eyes   lest   a   storm sur- prise;   We   will
sea- man's breast, courage   still   may   rest;   In   his

casts his lot with the sea, Finding for- tune free.
steer our swim- ming horse, Holding fast our course!
fist he holds his life, Fears but God in strife.

97. Never Weather-Beaten Sail

Thomas Campion (1567–1620), physician, poet, and composer, published this song in 1613. The fact that words and music come from the same pen gives the song exceptional calm and inner radiance.

Andantino

1. Ne-ver wea-ther beat-en sail more will-ing bent to shore,
   Ne-ver ti- réd pilgrim's limbs af- fec-ted slum-ber more

Than my wea-ried sprite now longs to fly out of my

trou- bled breast. O come quickly, O come quickly, O come quickly,

sweet-est Lord, and take my soul to rest.

2. Ever blooming are the joys of heav'n's high pa-ra-dise.
   Cold age deafs not there our ears, nor vapour dims our eyes;
   Glory there the sun outshines, whose beams the blessèd only see.
   O come quickly, O come quickly, O come quickly,
   Glorious Lord, and raise my sprite to thee.

98. Lord of the Universe, Hear my Prayer

Ancient Indian chant

The rhythm of this ancient chant may seem curious to Western ears, so it is best not to overthink the tempo – simply let it flow.

99. Non Nobis Domine

A canon in three parts by William Byrd

At the start of his career, William Byrd (1543–1623) was organist at Lincoln Cathedral, famous for its magnificent medieval 'Angel choir' carved on the spandrel of the triforium arcade.

ALL THREE VOICES
FINISH TOGETHER
AT THE PAUSE
(ADJUST WORDS AD LIB)

127

100. Come and Sing this Christmas Morn

A two-or three-part Polish carol

This carol derives from Polish folk tradition. Its rhythmic vigour and strident intervals require confident handling.

ev'- ry na-tion: Glo- ri- a,   Glo- ri- a

Glo-ria,   Glo-ria

Glo- ri- a   in ex- cel- sis   De ——

Glo- ria   in ex- cel- sis   De ——

2. Shepherds dance and spread the fame,
   That the angel choirs proclaim;
   Holy Night of Saviour's birth;
      Heaven born on earth.
   Angels' errand, shepherds singing:
   Man of good will, peace now bringing.
      Gloria, Gloria,
      Gloria, in excelsis Deo.

101. The Crown of Roses

Peter Ilich Tchaikovsky (1840–1893) encapsulates a profound inner drama in these words, translated from the Russian 'legend' by Plechtcheev. An average class orchestra can easily tackle a straightforward arrangement of it with a group holding the melodic line. Alternately, the full harmony may be found in the *Oxford Book of Carols*.

Then of the thorns they made a crown, And with rough fing-ers press'd it down, Till on his fore-head fair and young, Red drops of blood like ro- ses sprung.

102. Taquiriri

A Bolivian Huanyo

This song has been transcribed directly from Bolivian oral tradition, the roots of which go back to pre-Inca South America. It should bustle along quite quickly with an air of gossip, particularly in the last verse which can be sung with a cheeky smile.

Presto vivace

1. Ta-qui-ri-ri ly- su nya-ni-tay, Tu-su-ri-ri ly- su-un.
2. Charangoy wag-ha-san nya-ni-tay, Si-mi-si-tuy man-ta a
3. Noghapis wag-ha- ni nya-ni-tay, Nya-wi-si-tuy man-ta a.

CHORUS

Ay, chispa, chispa, nya- ni- tay, Lu-ri wanyu chispa a.

4. Ly ly ly ly ly ... etc.

103. I Gaze Out O'er the Moonlit Earth

A Breton carol

Two of Brittany's most famous associations are its relationship to the sea and its standing stones – sharp contrasts in many ways. The events in this song, taking place at the midnight hour within a cave, seem to arise naturally out of such a setting.

The crisp snow glit-ters on the ground.

2. So cold and sharp; and yet I know
   On such a winter night of old
   He came, the Holy Child, and lay
   In manger cradle, small and cold.

3. O light, once born in earth's dark night
   Make bright for us the path we tread,
   Our hearts make warm with thy great love
   Until our souls to thee are led.

104. Easter Eggs

A Russian chorus in three parts by Rimsky-Korsakov

The words in this chorus by Rimsky-Korsakov (1844–1908) are used throughout Russia as an Easter greeting. It first appeared in a popular collection of *Russian National Songs* in 1877.

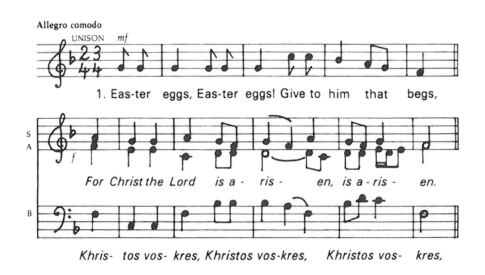

2. To the poor, open the door;
Something give of your store,

3. Those who hoard can't afford:
Moth and dust their reward,

4. Those who love, freely give,
Long and well may they live,

5. Eastertide, like a bride,
Comes and won't be denied,

105. 'Neath the Spreading Chestnut Branches

A round in four parts by Haydn

Breughel's famous picture of Flemish peasants at a wedding dance inspired the words of this round. Apart from the tricky, unexpected rests that are so typical of Haydn's musical humour, one can really let go in this relaxed mood of village merriment.

Ritmo di due battute

Poco forte e poco staccato

'Neath the spreading chestnut branches, Vil-lage folk are gay;

'Neath the spread of merry laughter, Greetings ring from floor to raf-ter

for the wedding day. Cheer up friends and cease your

moan- ing. Hear the spank-fat bagpipes dron-ing And the

white scrub'd
food-stack'd tables groaning; Cast care a- way!

Come in bright ar- ray. Take your part-ners for the

dancing; Fiddlers' elbows prancing; Join in the jig and skip in the fray;

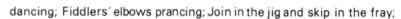

Sweethearts singing, twist-ing, clap-ping, Plea-ted skirts and

ap- rons wild-ly flap-ping in the hey.

135

106. All Through the Night

Ar Hyd y Nos

This is a traditional Welsh song, long connected with the beautiful vesper 'God that Madest Earth and Heaven'. Rather fittingly, the melody is grounded in the bass stave.

Andante con tenerezza

1. Fie- ry day is   e- ver mock-ing Man's fee-ble sight: Man's sight:
Dark-ness eve by eve un- lock-ing Heav'n's cas-ket

1. Fie- ry   day   is   e- ver mock-ing Man's fee-ble sight: Man's sight:
Dark-ness eve by   eve un- lock-ing Heav'n's cas-ket

1. Fie- ry   day   is   e- ver mock-ing Man's fee-ble sight ————————:
Dark-ness eve by   eve un- lock-ing Heav'n's cas-ket

bright. Heav'n's cas-ket   bright ——————————————

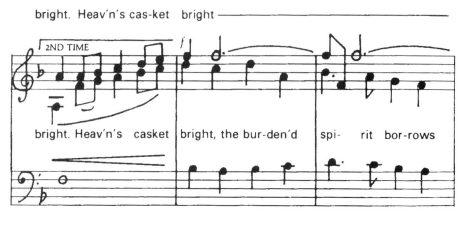

bright. Heav'n's   casket | bright, the bur-den'd | spi-   rit bor-rows

bright ———————————————. Thence the bur-den'd   spi-   rit bor-rows

Text above music (verse line 1):
.La- bo- rious mor- rows, Star-ry peace to

Text in staff (upper voice):
Strength to meet la- bo- rious mor- rows, Star- ry peace to

Text below first system (lower voice):
Strength to meet la- bo- rious mor- rows, Star- ry peace to

soothe his sor-rows, all through the night.

soothe his sor-rows, all through the night————.

soothe his sor-rows, all through the night————.

2. Planet after planet sparkling
　　All through the night,
　Down on earth their sister darkling,
　　Shed faithful light.
　In our mortal days declining
　　May our souls, as calmly shining,
　Cheer the restless and repining,
　　Till lost in sight.

107. Sumer is icumen in

This fourteenth-century piece, a round in twelve parts, is one of the treasures that has survived from Chaucer's times, shining like a beacon from the Middle Ages. The slight effort required to familiarise pupils with the language will always be richly rewarded.

108. Shalom Chaverim

Hebrew round in four parts

Shalom means 'peace', but can also be used as a greeting or farewell. The whole phrase together means 'Farewell friends, till we meet again' and is a beautiful way to end a recital or event.

Songs by Season and Theme

Harvest

21. The Merry Haymakers
24. Reap the Flax
46. Life from Dead Furrow

Michaelmas

2. Unconquered Hero of the Skies
68. Michaelmas Time
92. Firmly on the Earth I Stand

Christmas

6. The Shepherd's Song
26. Alleluia
27. The Song of Christmas Day
50. The Fire of Ash Twigs
52. O Holy Night
53. Three Kings Come Star-led Riding
70. Deo Gratias
72. Make We Merry
100. Come and Sing this Christmas Morn
103. I Gaze Out O'er the Moonlit Earth

New Year

28. New Year
73. Ring Out, Wild Bells

Spring

12. The Dawn Wind Now is Waking
16. How Delightful to See
32. A Sea Bird to her Chicks
82. The Streams in the Mountains

Easter

9. On this, our Glorious Eastertide
10. This Joyful Easter Day
31. Love is Come Again
33. Tomorrow Shall be my Dancing Day
56. Farewell Night
57. Easter Day
78. Pangue Lingua
79. Under the Leaves of Life
80. When Daffodils on Fields of Green
81. Why with Bulrush Mock Him?
101. The Crown of Roses
104. Easter Eggs

Summer

17. Once on a Bright Summer's Day
63. On the Hills the John-Fires Burn
107. Sumer is icumin in

Weddings

1. Step We Gaily
19. The Flowers in the Valley
105. 'Neath the Spreading Chestnut Branches

Birthdays

20. Waken Sleeping Butterfly
23. Happy Birthday

Foreign Language

18. The Ash Grove
32. A Sea Bird to her Chicks
48. Bhajan
49. Hail Light of Lights
61. Che Farò Senza Euridice?
78. Pangue Lingua
88. Anne de Bretagne
90. Michael Sea-Lord
94. Ein Feste Burg
98. Lord of the Universe, Hear my Prayer
99. Non Nobis Domine
108. Shalom Chaverim
102. Taquiriri

Index by Title, First Line and Composer

Acknowledgments

Floris Books acknowledges permissions for the following:

4. Heaven Blue
Music reproduced by permission of
Bärenreiter Verlag Kassel

6. The Shepherd's Song
Words from *Weft for the Rainbow*
by permission of Lanthorn Press

12. The Dawn Wind now is Waking
English words from the *Oxford Book of Carols*
by permission of Oxford University Press

13. Little Red Bird of the Lonely Moor
Music © Stainer & Bell Ltd. Reproduced by
permission.

14. Down in the Valley
Words from the *Oxford Book of Carols* by
permission of Oxford University Press

15. How Beautiful they are, the Lordly Ones
Words and music © Stainer & Bell Ltd.
Reproduced by permission.

22. Sigurd and the Dragon
English translation from *Folk Songs of
Europe* by permission of Maud Karpeles
and Novello & Co Ltd.

30. To Wander is the Miller's Joy
English translation reproduced by
permission of Oxford University Press

31. Love is Come Again
Words and music from the *Oxford Book of
Carols* by permission of Oxford University
Press

40. For All the Saints
Words and music reproduced by
permission of Oxford University Press

64. Migildi, Magildi
English translation reproduced by
permission of Oxford University Press

101. The Crown of Roses
English translation by G. Dearmer from the
Oxford Book of Carols by permission of
Oxford University Press

Further Reading

Early Years

Ellersiek, Wilma, *Dancing Hand, Trotting Pony: Hand Gesture Games, Songs and Movement Games for Children in Kindergarten and the Lower Grades*, WECAN

—, *Gesture Games for Spring and Summer: Hand Gesture, Song and Movement Games for Children in Kindergarten and the Lower Grades*, WECAN

—, *Gesture Games for Autumn and Winter: Hand Gesture, Song and Movement Games for Children in Kindergarten and the Lower Grades*, WECAN

—, *Gesture Games for Spring, Summer, Autumn and Winter: A Learning CD*, WECAN

—, *Giving Love, Bringing Joy: Hand Gesture Games and Lullabies in the Mood of the Fifth, for Children Between Birth and Nine*, WECAN

—, *Giving Love, Bringing Joy: A Learning CD*, WECAN

Foster, Nancy, The *Mood of the Fifth: A Musical Approach to Early Childhood*, WECAN

Lonsky, Karen, *A Day Full of Song (Book & CD)*, WECAN

Willwerth, Ilian, *Merrily We Sing: Original Songs in the Mood of the Fifth*, WECAN

Zahlingen, Bronja, *Lifetime of Joy: A Collection of Circle Games, Finger Games, Songs, Verses and Plays for Puppets and Marionettes*, WECAN

Lower School

Barnes, Diane Ingraham, *Music Through the Grades in the Light of the Developing Child*, Adonis Press

Bernstein, Steve, *Recorder Ensemble: First Collection for Soprano, Alto, Tenor and Bass*, Association of AWSNA

Bryer, Estelle, *The Rainbow Puppet Theater Book: Fourteen Classic Puppet Plays*, WECAN

Ellersiek, Wilma, *Nativity Plays for Children: Celebrating Christmas through Movement and Music*, Floris Books

Moore, Richard, *Five Plays for Waldorf Festivals*, Steiner Waldorf Schools Fellowship

Preston, Michael, *Music from Around the World for Recorders: Ensemble Music for Descant, Alto and Tenor Recorders in Waldorf Schools*, AWSNA

Spence, Roswitha, *Clothing the Play: The Art and Craft of Stage Design*, AWSNA

Taylor, Michael, *Finger Strings: A Book of Cat's Cradles and String Figures*, Floris Books

Wildgruber, Thomas, *Painting and Drawing in Steiner-Waldorf Schools: Classes 1-8*, Floris Books

Steiner-Waldorf Schools

In 2015 there are over 1000 Waldorf schools and 1,500 kindergartens in over 60 countries around the world. Up-to-date information can be found on any of the websites below.

AUSTRALIA
Steiner Education Australia
steinereducation.edu.au

NEW ZEALAND
Federation of Rudolf Steiner Schools
www.rudolfsteinerfederation.org.nz

SOUTH AFRICA
Southern African Federation of Waldorf Schools
www.waldorf.org.za

NORTH AMERICA
Association of Waldorf Schools of North America
www.whywaldorfworks.org

Waldorf Early Childhood Association of North America
www. waldorfearlychildhood.org

UK
Steiner Waldorf Schools Fellowship
www.steinerwaldorf.org.uk

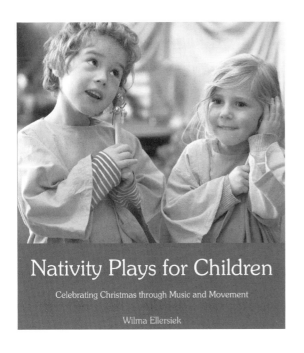

Nativity Plays for Children

Celebrating Christmas through Music and Movement

Wilma Ellersiek

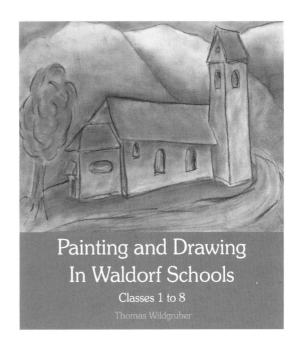

Painting and Drawing In Waldorf Schools

Classes 1 to 8

Thomas Wildgruber

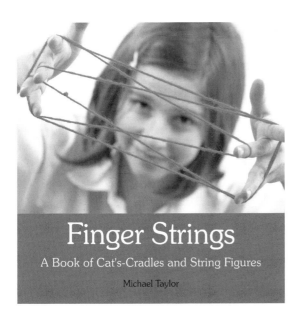

Finger Strings

A Book of Cat's-Cradles and String Figures

Michael Taylor

Magical Window Stars

Frédérique Guéret

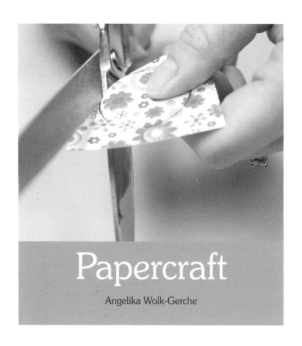

Papercraft

Angelika Wolk-Gerche

Earth, Water, Fire and Air

Playful Explorations in the Four Elements

Walter Kraul

Crafts Through the Year

Thomas and Petra Berger

Woodworking with Children

Anette Grunditz and Ulf Erixon

www.florisbooks.co.uk